KID WEALTH WIZARDS

The Ultimate NEEDS vs. WANTS WORKBOOK

AGES 4-8

INTERACTIVE LEARNING, SMART CHOICES, AND ENGAGING GAMES FOR HOME AND CLASSROOM

The Ultimate
NEEDS VS. WANTS
WORKBOOK

To the young wizards of tomorrow, Within these pages lies a map, not of hidden treasures, but of knowledge. Learn its lessons well, and see how bright your future can be!

ISBN-13: 978-1-962550-14-7

Created by: O. Duggan
Published by: Kid Wealth Wizards Publishing
New York, USA
www.kidwealthwizards.com

This is a work of fiction. Any names, characters, businesses, locations, or events are purely the creation of the author or used fictitiously. Any resemblance to actual persons, living or dead, or real events is purely coincidental.

WWW.KIDWEALTHWIZARDS.COM

THIS BOOK BELONGS TO

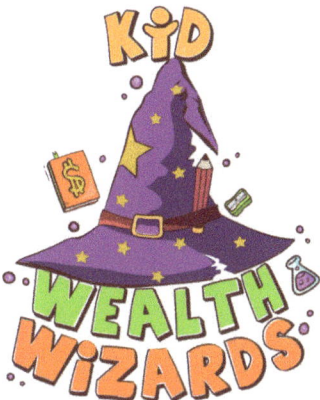

Table of Contents

Section 1: Introduction

Section 2: Activity Pages

Section 3: Coloring Pages

Section 4: Lessons & Quiz Pages

Section 5: Review and Achievement

Introduction of Needs and Wants

Hi kids! Today, we're going to learn about two important words: needs and wants.
A need is something you must have to live and be healthy.

Think about things like food, water, a place to live, and clothes to keep you warm.

Needs

A want is something that you would like to have, but you don't need it to live. These are things like toys, candy, or a trip to the zoo.

Let's remember: needs help us live, and wants make us happy but are not necessary for living.

Wants

Connect the Dots - Discover Needs and Wants

Connect the dots to discover which items are needs and which are wants. Can you tell which ones we really need to live well and which ones are just for fun?

Needs Wants

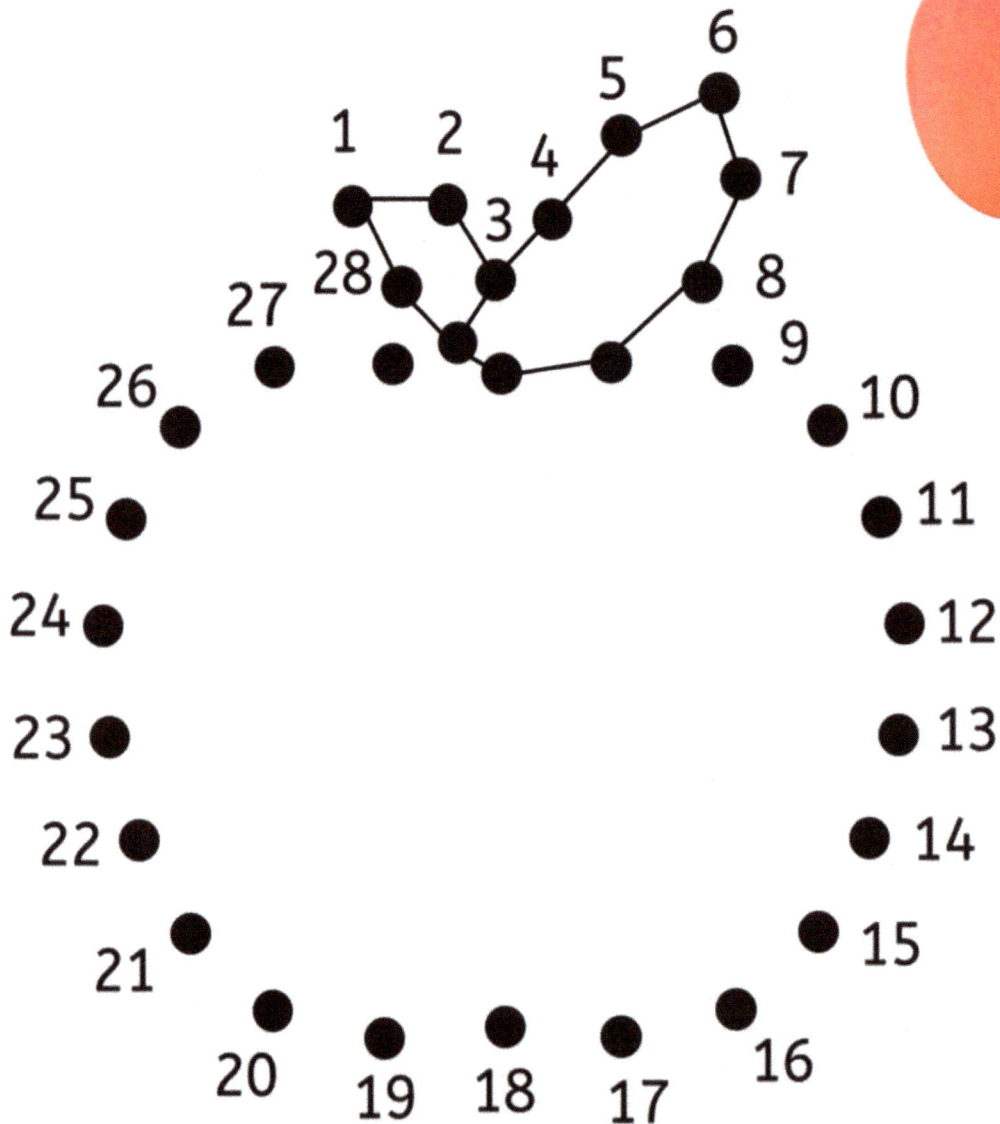

3.

Needs Wants

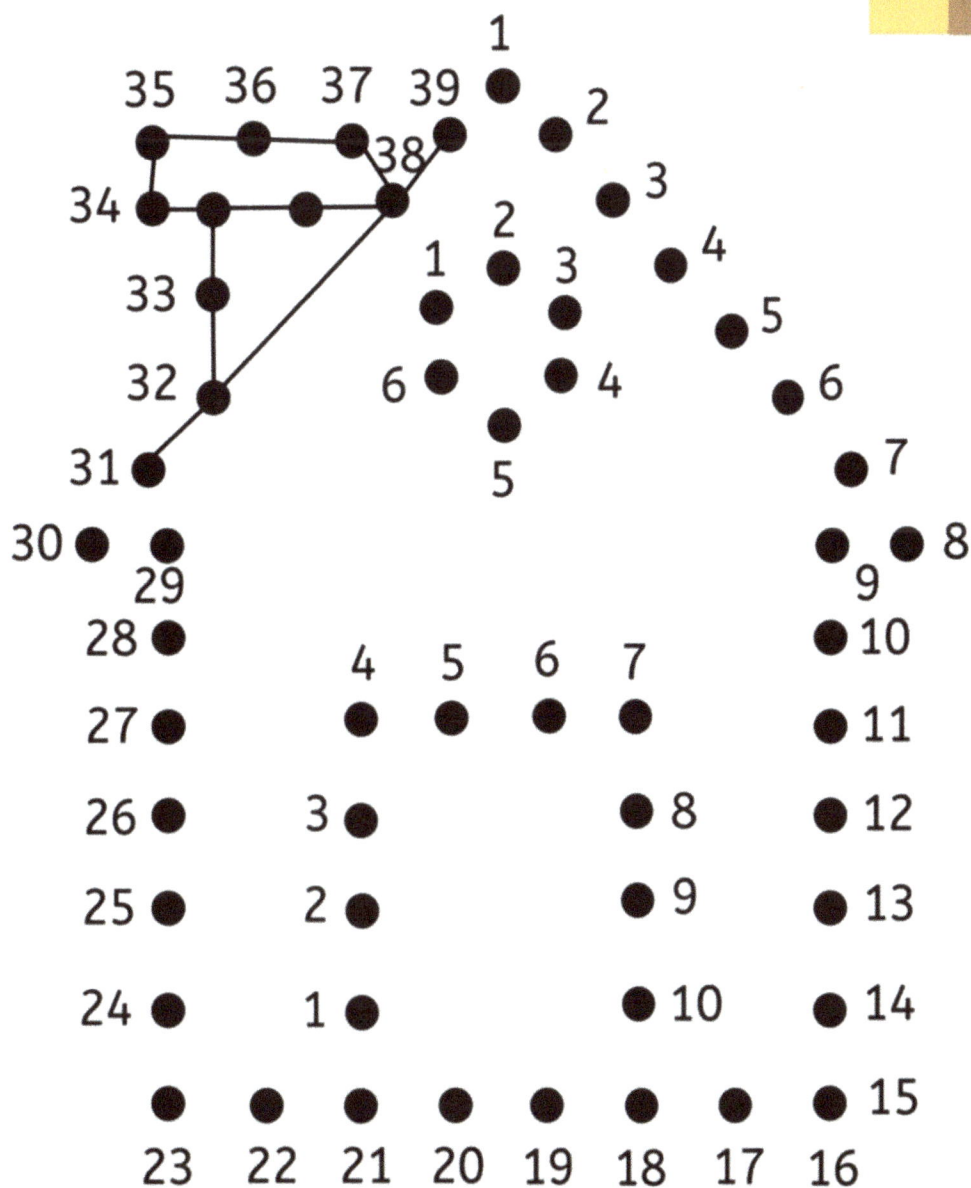

Needs Wants

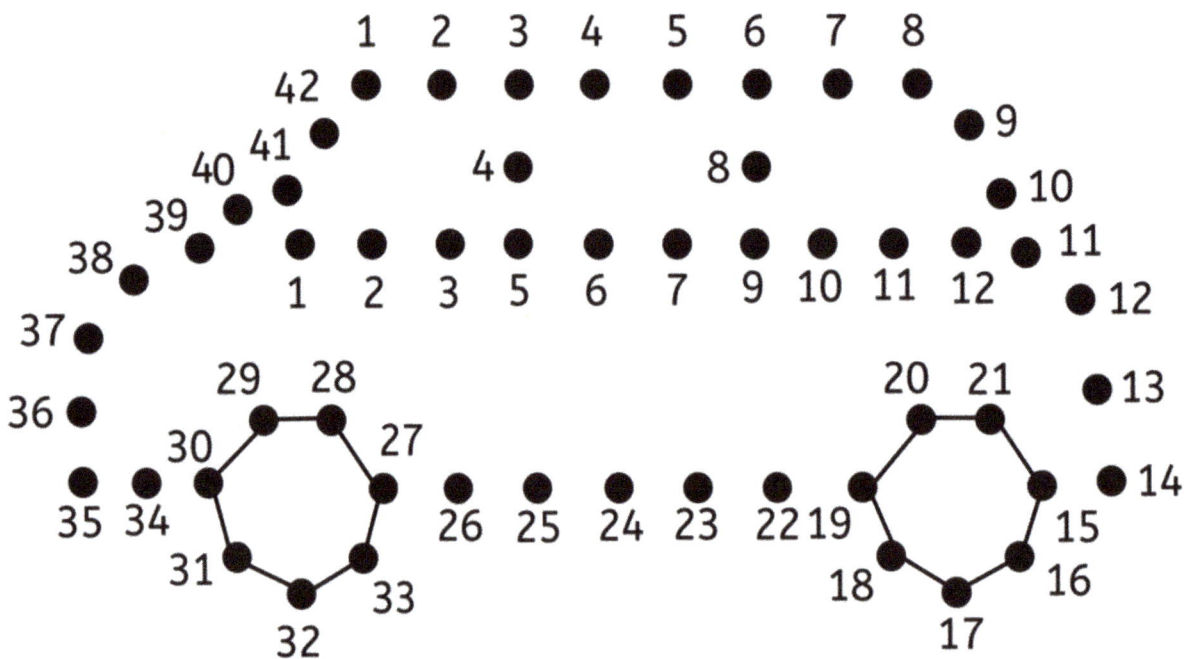

Needs Wants

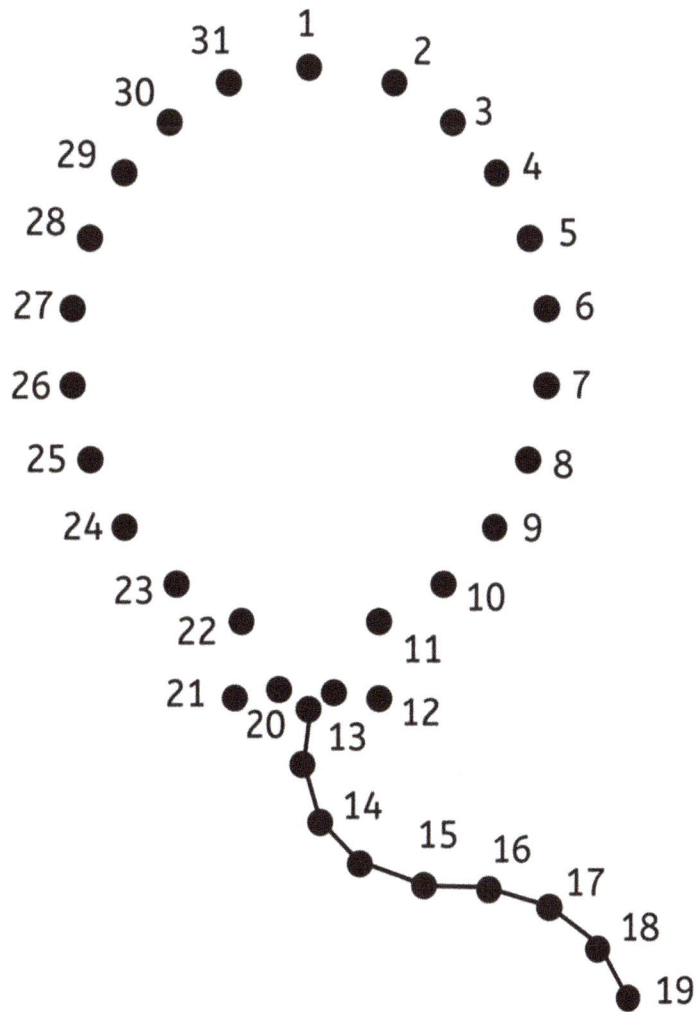

Categorizing Needs and Wants

Draw a line from each item to the correct category:
Need or Want.

NEEDS

WANTS

NEEDS

WANTS

Draw Your Own Needs and Wants

We all need certain things to live well, like food and a home. We also all have things we wish we had because they make us happy. Can you draw one thing you really need and one thing you really want? Then, tell us why you chose them!

Something I Need

_____

_____

_____

9. _____

Something I Want

_____

_____

_____

_____

Color the Needs

Here are some things we all need to live well every day.
Can you color these important items?

Use your favorite colors to bring them to life!

Apples keep you
healthy and strong.

Water helps you
stay hydrated.

A house keeps you
safe from the weather.

Clothes keep you
warm and protected.

Color the Wants

Here are some things that are fun to have but we don't need them to live well. Can you color these exciting items?

Choose bright and happy colors to make them look fun!

Toy cars can zoom around, making playtime exciting!

Cupcakes are a sweet treat for special occasions!

Video games can be fun when played with friends!

Roller skates help you glide and spin around!

Color and Sort the Items

Here are some everyday things. Color them and then decide if they are something we really need or just something nice to have.

Draw a line from each item to the correct basket labeled 'Needs' or 'Wants.

Ice cream

Banana

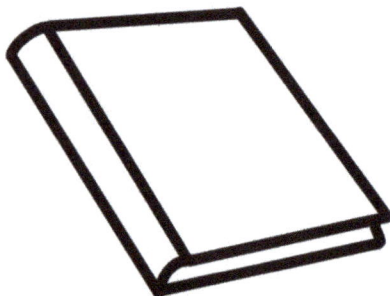

Book

Ball

Teddy bear

Needs

Toothbrush

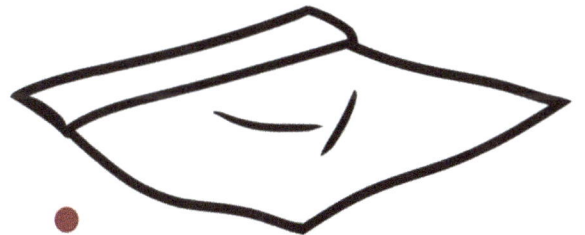

Blanket

Wants

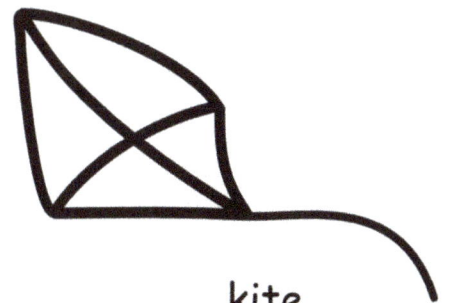

kite

Needs vs. Wants Scenarios

Read each scenario and decide
if it's a need or a want.
Circle your answer next to each scenario.

Lila is thirsty after playing outside. She asks her mom for a glass of water.

NEEDS   WANTS

Tom sees a new toy truck in the store and asks his dad if he can have it.

NEEDS   WANTS

Mia's shoes are too small and hurt her feet. She needs new shoes that fit.

NEEDS   WANTS

Jack wants a piece of chocolate after dinner.

NEEDS   WANTS

Sara's family needs to buy groceries for the week.

NEEDS   WANTS

What I Learned

Think about everything you've learned about needs and wants. Below, draw a picture of one thing you really need and one thing you really want. Then, explaining why you chose each item.

Something I Need

Think about something you use every day!

_____

_____

_____

_____

Something I Want

What is something fun you love to play with?

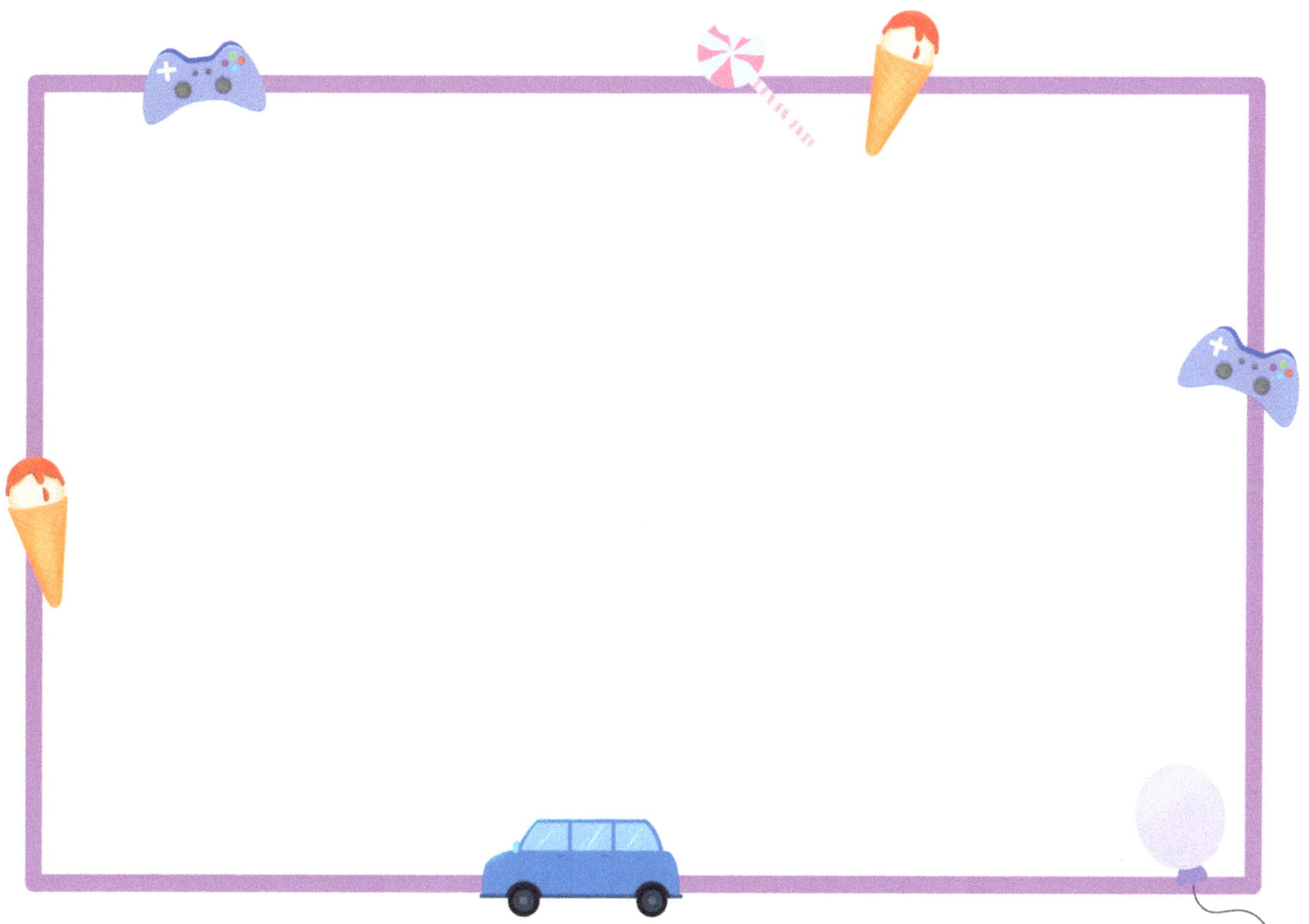

Wants vs. Needs: Life Edition for Kids

Look at the list of things below. Some of these are things we need to live, and some are just for fun.

Can you help sort them into the right list?

1.

Fresh water

2.

Home

3.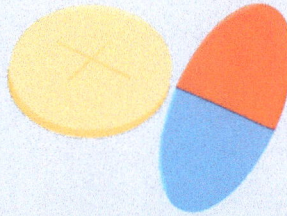

Medicine

4.

Shoes

5.

Bread

6.

Teddy bear

7.

Candy

8.

Skateboard

9.

TV

10.

Balloons

You Sort List

Needs   Wants

_____   _____

_____   _____

_____   _____

_____   _____

_____   _____

Wants vs. Needs: School Supplies Edition

Time to prepare for school! There are items you definitely need for school and some that would be nice but not necessary.

Can you categorize them?

1.

Pencil

2.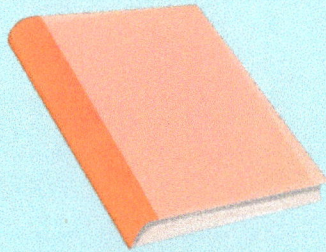

Notebook

3.

Backpack

4.

Textbook

5.

Calculator

6.

Stickers

7.

Action figure

8.

Candy

9.

Poster of favorite singer

10.

Trading cards

You Sort List

School Needs

_____

_____

_____

_____

_____

School Wants

_____

_____

_____

_____

_____

Wants vs. Needs: Island Adventure

Imagine you're on an exciting island adventure!
Some things are very important because you need them
to be safe and healthy (these are "Needs").

Other things are just fun to have but aren't necessary
for your safety (these are "Wants").

Can you help sort them into the right list?

1.

Fresh water

2.

Toy Car

3.

Playstation

4.

Sunscreen

5.

Healthy food

6.
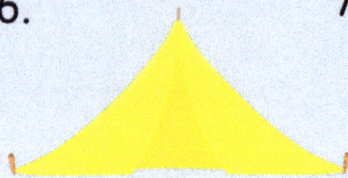
Tent

7.

Drawing kit

8.

Stuffed animal

9.

First aid kit

10.

Ice cream cone

23.

You Sort List

Island Needs

_____

_____

_____

_____

_____

Island Wants

_____

_____

_____

_____

_____

Needs vs. Wants
Scavenger Hunt

Let's go on an exciting scavenger hunt! Can you find these items in your home or classroom?

Draw a picture of each item you find and place it in the right category.

Needs

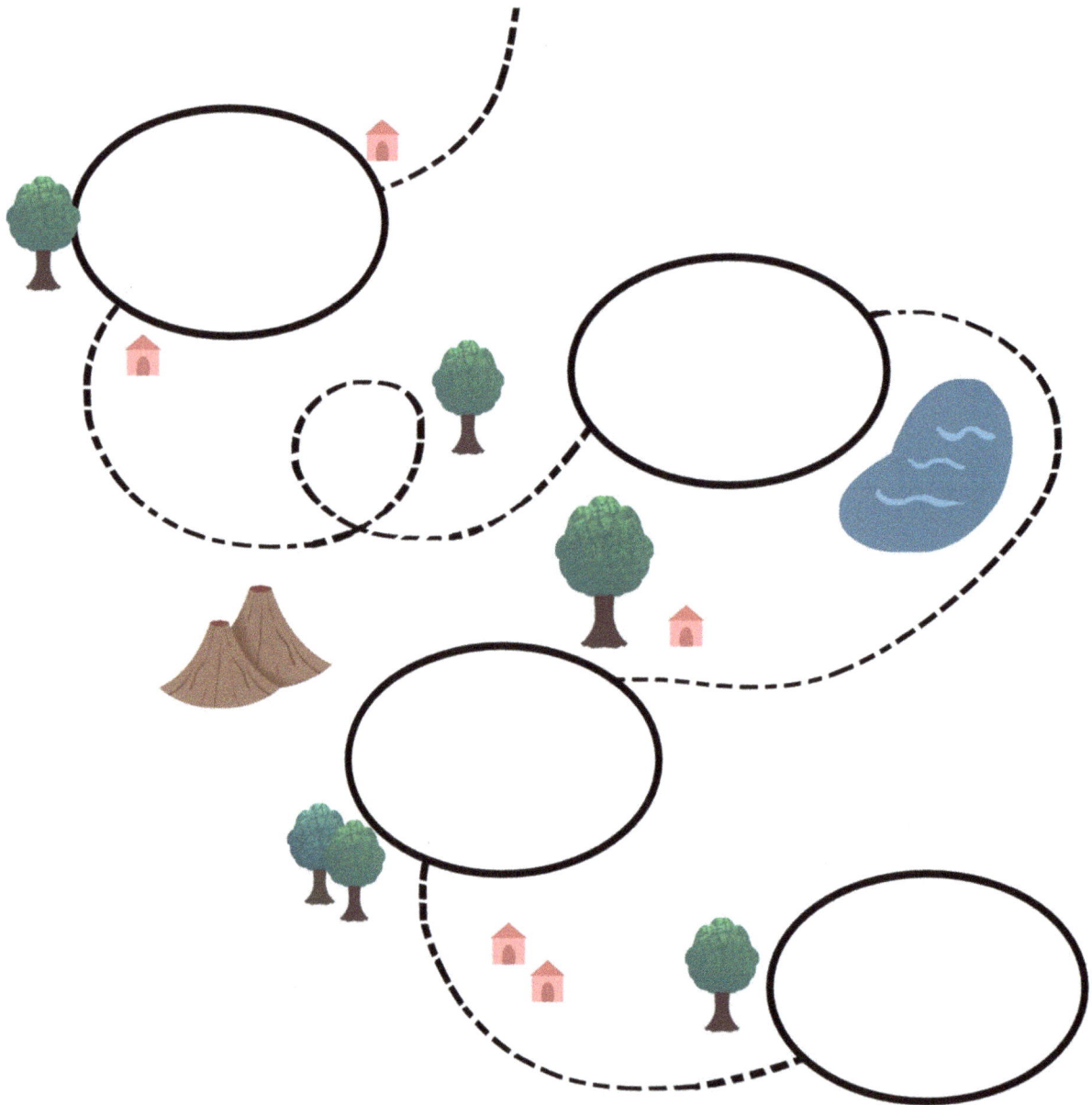

Wants

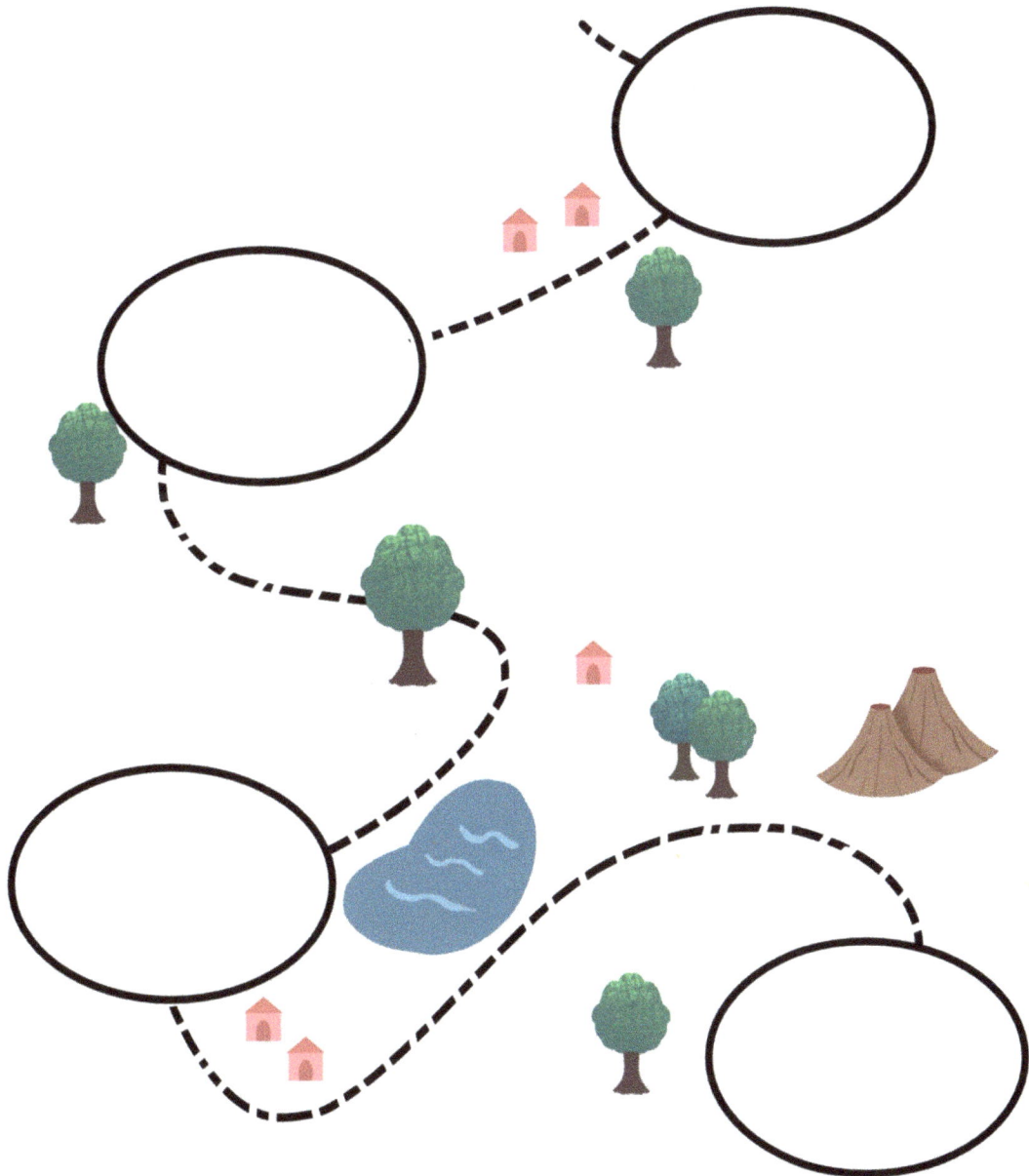

Needs vs. Wants Quiz

Let's see how much you remember! Circle the correct answer for each question below.

Is it a 'Need' (something very important for everyone) or a 'Want' (something nice to have but not necessary)?

Is water a need or a want? 💧

Is a toy a need or a want? 🚙

Is food a need or a want? 🍲

Is a new iPad or Tablet a need or a want?

Is a house a need or a want?

Review Your Achievement

Congratulations, Young Explorer!

You did it! You've completed the Wants vs. Needs Adventure. You're now an expert at knowing the difference between what we need to live and what we like to have for fun. Great job!

Certificate of Achievement

This certifies that _____
has successfully completed the Wants vs.
Needs Adventure and is now a Wants vs.
Needs Expert!

Signed: _____
Date: _____

Needs vs. Wants
Workbook Answer Key

Page 3-6: Connect the Dots

Needs:

1. Apple: Apples are food that helps us stay healthy.
2. House: A house is where we live and stay safe.

Wants:

3. Toy Car: Toy cars are fun to play with but we don't need them to live.
4. Balloon: Balloons are fun and make us happy, but we don't need them to live.

Page 7-8: Categorizing Needs and Wants

Needs:

5. Apple: We need food like apples to stay healthy.
6. Water Bottle: We need water to drink every day.
7. House: We need a place to live to be safe.
8. Shirt: We need clothes to keep us warm.

Wants:

9. Toy Car: Toys are fun but we don't need them to live.
10. Candy: Candy tastes good, but we don't need it to stay healthy.
11. Balloon: Balloons are fun but not necessary for living.
12. Game Controller: Video games are fun, but we don't need them to live.

Page 9-10: Draw Your Own Needs and Wants

(Answers will vary based on children's drawings and explanations)

Page 11: Color the Needs

Items to Color:

1. Apple: Apples are food that helps us stay healthy.
2. Water Bottle: We need water to drink every day.
3. House: A house is where we live and stay safe.
4. Shirt: We need clothes to keep us warm.

Page 12: Color the Wants

Items to Color:

5. Toy Car: Toy cars are fun to play with but we don't need them to live.
6. Cupcake: Cupcakes are treats that taste good, but we don't need them.
7. Video Game Controller: Playing video games is fun, but we don't need it.
8. Roller Skates: Roller skates are fun for playing, but not necessary.

Page 13-14: Color and Sort the Items

Needs:

1. Banana: Bananas are food that helps us stay healthy.
2. Toothbrush: We need a toothbrush to keep our teeth clean.
3. Blanket: A blanket keeps us warm when we sleep.
4. Book: Books help us learn new things.

Wants:

5. Soccer Ball: Soccer balls are fun to play with but not needed to live.
6. Ice Cream Cone: Ice cream is a tasty treat but not necessary.
7. Kite: Kites are fun to fly but we don't need them.
8. Stuffed Animal: Stuffed animals are nice to cuddle, but we don't need them.

Page 15-16: Needs vs. Wants Scenarios

9. Lila asks for a glass of water: Need. We need water to stay healthy.
10. Tom asks for a toy truck: Want. Toys are fun but not needed to live.
11. Mia needs new shoes: Need. Shoes protect our feet and help us walk.
12. Jack wants a piece of chocolate: Want. Chocolate tastes good, but we don't need it to stay healthy.
13. Sara's family needs to buy groceries: Need. We need food to eat every day.

Page 19-20: Wants vs. Needs: Life Edition for Kids

Needs:

1. Fresh Water: We need water to drink every day.
2. Home: We need a place to live to be safe.
3. Medicine: Medicine helps us get better when we're sick.
4. Shoes: Shoes protect our feet and help us walk.
5. Bread: Bread is food that helps us stay healthy.

Wants:

6. Teddy Bear: Teddy bears are nice to cuddle, but we don't need them.
7. Candy: Candy tastes good, but we don't need it to stay healthy.
8. Skateboard: Skateboards are fun to play with but not needed to live.
9. TV: Watching TV is fun, but we don't need it to live.
10. Balloons: Balloons are fun but not necessary for living.

Page 21-22: Wants vs. Needs: School Supplies Edition

School Needs:

1. Pencil: We need pencils to write and draw.
2. Notebook: We need notebooks to write down what we learn.
3. Backpack: We need backpacks to carry our school supplies.
4. Textbook: We need textbooks to help us learn.
5. Calculator: Calculators help us with math.

School Wants:

6. Stickers: Stickers are fun to use but not needed.
7. Action Figure: Action figures are fun to play with but not needed.
8. Candy: Candy tastes good, but we don't need it for school.
9. Poster of Favorite Singer: Posters are fun to look at but not needed.
10. Trading Cards: Trading cards are fun to collect but not needed.

Page 23-24: Wants vs. Needs: Island Adventure

Survival Needs:

1. Fresh Water: We need water to drink to stay alive.
2. Tent: We need shelter to stay safe and dry.
3. First Aid Kit: We need a first aid kit to help us if we get hurt.
4. Sunscreen: Sunscreen protects our skin from the sun.
5. Healthy Food: We need food to eat to stay healthy.

Island Wants (Extras):

6. Toy Car: Toy cars are fun to play with but not needed.
7. Playstation: Playstations are fun to use but not needed.
8. Drawing Kit: Drawing kits are fun for art but not needed.
9. Stuffed Animal: Stuffed animals are nice to cuddle but not needed.
10. Ice Cream Cone: Ice cream is a tasty treat but not necessary.

Page 27-28: Needs vs. Wants Quiz

1. Is water a need or a want?

   Need. We need water to stay healthy.

2. Is a toy a need or a want?

   Want. Toys are fun but not needed to live.

3. Is food a need or a want?

   Need. We need food to stay healthy.

4. Is a new iPad or Tablet a need or a want?

   Want. Tablets are fun but not needed to live.

5. Is a house a need or a want?

   Need. We need a place to live to be safe.